Poems of the Moment

Edited by Scott Tilley

Poems of the Moment

Cover design © Scott Tilley

Published by Precious Poetry

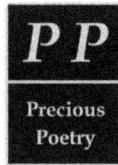

P P

Precious
Poetry

An imprint of Precious Publishing, LLC

Precious Publishing
www.PreciousPublishing.biz

ISBN-13: 978-1-951750-13-8
ISBN-13: 978-1-951750-14-5 (ebook)

TABLE OF CONTENTS

Part III: Gratitude   **33**

Part VI: Spring Forward   85

DEDICATION

To Sam, Salvador, Dave, Grace, and John.

Each of you has left a distinct impression, contributing in a uniquely personal manner. Together, you helped weave the vibrant threads that form the rich tapestry of this anthology.

PREFACE

In the fleeting moments of our days, where time often slips unnoticed, poetry can capture the essence of life's ephemeral beauty. *Poems of the Moment* is an anthology that aspires to do just that: to hold the transient, to appreciate the unnoticed, and to celebrate the ordinary yet extraordinary facets of daily life.

This collection is an assembly of words and a mosaic of moments. Each poem reflects the diverse rhythms of the human experience and resonates with the seasons of the year and the emotions of the heart. From the quiet contemplation of Thanksgiving to the playful mischief of April Fools, these poems traverse a landscape rich in emotion and imagery.

As you turn these pages, I hope you discover echoes of your own experiences and thoughts that have lingered, unspoken. This book is more than a journey through the calendar – it's a celebration of the brief instances that etch a lasting imprint on our souls.

Let this anthology serve as a companion in your quieter times, a friend to accompany you in reflection, and a reminder of the beauty in the here and now. May these poems resonate with you, offering comfort, inspiration, and a renewed appreciation for the poetry that lives in every moment of our lives.

Welcome to this journey through time and emotion. Welcome to *Poems of the Moment.*

Scott Tilley
Melbourne, FL
December 30, 2023

Acknowledgments

As *Poems of the Moment* finds its way into the world, my heart brims with gratitude for the many who have journeyed with me in bringing this anthology to life.

To the circle of poets who attended our meetings, your contributions have been the very heartbeat of this project. Your diverse voices, rich with emotion and insight, have woven a tapestry of words that breathes life into every page. Your commitment, creativity, and camaraderie have been the pillars upon which this anthology stands. Any errors remaining in the text are solely my responsibility.

Thanks to the Florida Institute of Technology Alumni Center and the West Melbourne Public Library, our sanctuaries and creative hubs. Your welcoming spaces housed our meetings and nurtured a sense of community and belonging. Your support helped guide this collective endeavor from a mere concept to a tangible reality.

I am profoundly indebted to wordsmiths throughout history whose timeless works have inspired me. Your verses have traversed time and space, reminding us that the human experience is universal and enduring. You have been invaluable mentors.

To my beloved pets at home, you have been my silent companions through this journey. In your unique ways, you have provided comfort, laughter, and a calming presence that often cleared the fog on challenging days. Your unconditional love and quirky antics have been a source of joy and jollity.

Lastly, to every reader who embarks on this poetic journey, may these poems touch your heart and stir your soul, as they have mine.

Precious Publishing Academy – September 3, 2022

1:00pm - 3:00pm at FIT Alumni Center in Melbourne, FL

Technology, the Art of Writing, and the Business of Publishing

Precious Publishing
www.PreciousPublishing.biz

Academy

Anthology
Alliance

CTS
Press

- Courses
- Webinars
- Workshops

Poetry – A Labor of Love

The Merriam-Webster dictionary defines the phrase *labor of love* as "a labor voluntarily undertaken or performed without consideration of any benefit or reward." In the case of **poetry**, monetary rewards and benefits are often few and far between. But the non-monetary rewards and benefits are innumerable. This Labor Day weekend, please join us in celebrating the creativity of poets, the beauty of poems, and the joy of reading or listening to these unique works of art.

The FIT Alumni Center is at 2600 Country Club Rd, Melbourne, FL 32901. There is free parking beside the Center. Contact Scott Tilley at stilley@preciouspublishing.biz or (321) 604-1294.

***

Speakers

Kit (Christopher Robin) Adams has been writing stories, essays, and poems since 1958. His writings have been published in journals from England to Hawaii, California to Florida. His poetry readings in Missouri and Florida have been well received. He retired from teaching English in Brevard County and Florida Virtual School and was a mentor with the National Writing Project. He was vice president of the Space Coast Writers' Guild and is president of the Brevard Scribblers. His first poetry collection, *Spanish Cedar: Preserving the ART of the Cigar Experience*, appeared in March 2014.

Scott Tilley is president and founder of Precious Publishing, an emeritus professor at the Florida Institute of Technology, president and founder of the Center for Technology & Society, president and co-founder of Big Data Florida, Senior Fellow at the American Security Council Foundation, past president of INCOSE Space Coast, and a Space Coast Writers' Guild Fellow. His recent books include *AFTERMATH* (2022), *PETS* (2021), and *PANDEMIC* (2020). He holds a Ph.D. in computer science from the University of Victoria.

www.PreciousPublishing.biz/join

LABOR OF LOVE

Christopher Robin Adams

"Without expectation of reward."
That's the phrase meaning.
Still, I can't tell you
                or anyone
how or what to write,
even for gold.
Here, poetically,
if you like what you hear,
                use it.
Allow its presence to touch you,
to caress your heart
        or tighten your sphincter.
If ice meets your spine,
allow it to travel
both up and down;
it will find a track,
        if allowed.
Should nothing reach
as far as your cushioned chair,
fine.
It wasn't meant to be.
However, remember:
poetry is work
with little cold-hard reward.
It's love.

Part I: A Labor of Love

When I love,
I stretch.
I reach out, grab hold, and hang on.
Poetry is labor,
but I respect the labor
because I crave the results:
> learning about my being;
>> only then do I find my capabilities,
>> and only then can I fully help others.

We are Star Beings.
About nine percent of our bodies is hydrogen,
the same hydrogen
that creation burst out three billion years ago.
The explosion which gave us stars
and planets and asteroids,
also donated us to the universe.
Element-wise,
we can trace our lives to the beginning of time.
This massive idea,
very factual and solid,
gives me pause.

A long pause.
Some folks found gods
> to explain all;
others just dispensed with hows and whys
and concerned themselves
with their fellow Stardust beings:
> Is she hungry?
> Does he need shelter?
> Should we take it to an animal hospital?

Part I: A Labor of Love

All of us have lived together,
    held here by gravity,
and have grown closer together
    for millennium.
So,
stuck in the present,
we labor to understand
how to use and care for our Star-dust selves,
our families, and communities.

I use poetry
to find knowledge that puts ice in my spine,
passion in every cell of my body,
and pity deep in my heart
    for knowing others suffer.
I use poetry
as a mercy ship to do this,
to activate curiosity,
to serve justice,
to mobilize a humble love.

Let's breathe
    as One,
freshen the cranium content
with oxygen and many, many bits of nitrogen,
and discover more what we are,
who we are,
and what we can do on our tiny spinning globe
of rock, water, and its sliver of air.

Part I: A Labor of Love

As we think of labor,
let's ponder the depths of love
and examine poetry;
After all,
according to Matthew Arnold,
poetry offers us
the most concise
and clearest exposition
of all literature.

We must shift boxes of paradigms in our brains
and mix up our order.
it will stir dust,
make us sneeze and blink,
        but motes will settle.
We can then see, then hold loved ones
        who sparkle as newborn Stars
        but closer
in our arms
and clearer in our hearts.

Today, all our labor
        pauses;
we appreciate the form,
the shape,
the worthiness of understanding,
and the radiance of love shining through
        all we write.

# # #

A POET'S LAMENT

Peggy Ball

Writing a poem
Is not always easy;
Words may gush out,
Fluent and breezy,

Or they are hesitant,
Clogging your mind,
While you struggle and strain
To make the lines rhyme.

Keep pen and paper
Next to your bed
To record good ideas
That pop into your head

If a wonderful phrase
Attacks in the night:
Write it down quick;
It will die in the light.

When brilliant themes strike
And seem well-born,
Mull them over with care;
They might be just corn.

If you're lucky, your words
Will dance on the page

Part I: A Labor of Love

And make your heart young,
No matter your age.

There's pain and pleasure
 In being a poet,
It's labor and love,
And all wordsmiths know it.

# # #

ALL YOU NEED TO KNOW ABOUT LOVE

Peggy Ball

The mysteries of love have been studied for ages
By oracles, wisemen, gurus, and sages.

They've discovered convictions and contradictions
And even a few unwanted addictions.

They've learned that love is a mental condition
That may never fade to wholesome remission.

Happy or sad, or dreamy and yearning,
Love can be tender or lusty and burning,

Playful, euphoric, or wistful, or charming,
Smart as you are, it can be quite disarming.

If love is attacking, you may be coping,
But to find a sure cure, you are desperately hoping.

Never succumb and do not cower;
Just heed that old maxim: Go take a cold shower!

# # #

A LABOR OF LOVE

Betty Whitaker Jackson

His eyes are dim, his gait is slow
It's not too hard to reckon
That someday soon, we've got to know
He'll no longer answer our beckons.

I help him up, prepare soft meals
As a duty, I clean up his messes,
I can only imagine how he awful he feels
Dependent on me for "God's blesses."

A faithful companion all of these years
He's never complained or annoyed us,
To lose him will bring us buckets of tears
Missing his purrs, his loving caresses.

Old Zach is a feature, he runs the place
He's sort of a silent professor
We tell him our troubles, to his white-whiskered face,
Never judging, he just makes things better.

If only people could be like that cat
And live and let live and just listen
The world would be better, we so need all that,
He's heard our complaints, and dismissed 'em.

Part I: A Labor of Love

So, we'll love him 'til he's suffering pain
And know when it's time to dismiss him
To cat heaven , but in our hearts he'll remain
He labored to love us — we'll miss him.

# # #

MY FIRST RECITAL

Betty Whitaker Jackson

With all the confidence of a Carnegie Hall regular,
Little Kaley steps up to the platform
Planting her ruffled-socked feet just so.

Her left-side locks locked in a braid
(No free-flowing blond bouncy hair here),
She tucks her tiny violin in place.

Hand poised, fingers curved just so,
She places mid-bow, bow-hold as taught,
Poised, composed, she's ready to play.

Anticipation reigns. Patience must wait.
Introduction, when will it end?
It's time!

"Lightly Row, Lightly Row
O'er the glassy waves we go!"
Thirteen memorized notes she plays.

Repeat
"Smoothly glide, smoothly glide,
On the silent tide."
One-three-five-five, three.

Next, the refrain.
One-two-three-four-five same note,

Part I: A Labor of Love

Down-up-down-up-down, one note higher,

"Lightly row, lightly row"
One-three-five-five-three-three-three.
Rest position, bow down, finished!

Sweet "I did it" smile, a look at mom,
And that signature Suzuki from-the-waist bow,
Count to three.

Applause, applause, and flower bouquets
Family dinner to celebrate
That a star is born.

# # #

Previously published in *Encore: An Anthology of Stories and Poems* (2018) and used here with permission.

ELEGANCE EMPEARLED

Richard Marschall

I have never felt such compassion before!
Your letter is such an outpouring of love!
Your sentiments are lovely, like the sea to the shore.

Your parchment - fine, I love how your words pour!
I am lifted and cradled by the wings of a dove -
I have never felt such compassion before!

The hours you must have spent preparing its core -
every word from Jehovah's, heavens above.
Your sentiments are lovely, like the sea to the shore.

I thank you from my heart. I'm changed evermore!
Your gift, it is, magic, and most surely, true love!
I have never felt such compassion before!

Your thoughts, your pleas, the words you implore,
precious words, that I, could have never thought of.
Your sentiments are lovely, like the sea to the shore!

Men smarter than us, build golden altars and doors,
creating escapes, egress from death, undreamt of.
I have never felt such compassion before!
Your sentiments are lovely, like the sea to the shore!

# # #

THE ENJOYMENT OF WORK

Ashley McGrath

If you want to feel real joy,
Do a project you enjoy.
Completing a delayed task
Is something in which to bask.

Satisfaction is the reward
When your handiwork is adored.
You can be proud of
A labor of love.

# # #

Precious Publishing Academy – October 22, 2022
1:00pm - 3:00pm at FIT Alumni Center in Melbourne, FL

Technology, the Art of Writing, and the Business of Publishing

Precious Publishing
www.PreciousPublishing.biz

Academy

Anthology Alliance   **CTS Press**

• Courses   • Webinars   • Workshops

Poetry – Seriously Scary Stanzas

Our poetry series continues in October with a focus on Halloween and all things ominous and creepy. "The Raven" by Edgar Allan Poe was first published in January 1845. It's one of the best-known examples of a narrative poem relying on sadness, tragedy, and unexplained visits by harbingers of doom – in this case, the historically and culturally significant figure of the mysterious talking crow.

Once upon a midnight dreary, while I pondered, weak and weary,
Over many a quaint and curious volume of forgotten lore—
   While I nodded, nearly napping, suddenly there came a tapping,
As of some one gently rapping, rapping at my chamber door.
"'Tis some visitor," I muttered, "tapping at my chamber door—
   Only this and nothing more."

This won't be "Mickey's Not-So-Scary Halloween Party" (sold out for 2022) – it will be better! It's an opportunity to express your spookiest thoughts via scary stanzas. Dust off your costume, bring your favorite candy, and get your Poe on! Come ready to listen, write, and terrify your neighbors.

The FIT Alumni Center is at 2600 Country Club Rd, Melbourne, FL 32901. There is free parking beside the Center. Contact Scott Tilley at stilley@preciouspublishing.biz or (321) 604-1294.

***

Scott Tilley is president and founder of Precious Publishing, an emeritus professor at the Florida Institute of Technology, president and founder of the Center for Technology & Society, president and co-founder of Big Data Florida, Senior Fellow at the American Security Council Foundation, past president of INCOSE Space Coast, and a Space Coast Writers' Guild Fellow. His recent books include *AFTERMATH* (2022), *PETS* (2021), and *PANDEMIC* (2020). He holds a Ph.D. in computer science from the University of Victoria.

www.PreciousPublishing.biz/join

BEING IN YOUR PRESENCE

Christopher Robin Adams

In many dark nights,
you have flown into my thoughts;
light, airy, so crystalline with stars
that I would think they reflect off of you,
and yet – in the darkest of shadows,
in days when sun's set,
  sun's rising
  brackets the cloud-morphed day,
and you drop in
surprising my expectations of being alone.
A flower,
  colorful nowenthen
  and just running the roots at other times,
I had grown up with
  being alone
until you fluttered,
  lit upon a branch close by,
  startling my reverie.
Now,
even knowing you rest near,
I boggle at the light,
  at the seeming insubstantial
that carries so much
  gives so much
  provides so much to me.

#

16

BAD DREAM

Peggy Ball

I see
Scary black shapes
Floating through my window;
They come closer, and I wake up
Screaming.

# # #

GHOST RIDERS

Peggy Ball

Horses
With ghost riders
Thunder through the dark sky.
Their message is a chill warning;
Take heed!

# # #

RESCUED

Peggy Ball

The ghost
Is having fun
Scaring little children.
"Mom, come quick and turn on the light!"
Whew! Saved.

# # #

THE END

Peggy Ball

The house
Is dark inside;
I'm trembling in the gloom.
OH! It's not a house, it's a tomb!
Heart stops.

# # #

GOING BATTY

Peggy Insula

Flutter, flutter, little bat;
Come out, come out, wherever you're at.
Don't even try to take to flight.
I watched the cat drag you in tonight.

If you're hiding under the bed,
You'll only get dust bunnies on your head.
The cat's gone out on another prowl;
You're not likely to run afoul.

Never think that the bubbling stew
Steaming on my stove is waiting for you.
I'm not adding your juicy flesh
To my concoction of roadkill fresh.

I'm not planning to skin your wings
And drop them in with other things
Like mince of toad and tail of rat.
Come out, come out, wherever you're at.

# # #

SURPRISE IN THE SWAMP

Peggy Insula

Spanish moss shivered in the blood-red moon;
The dark silence split with the wail of a loon.
The swamp water burbled and spit green scum,
The murky water heaved, a voice growled, "Come!"

Something 'neath the nasty water lurked and stalled;
A black claw slithered out, snatched my head bald.
Spewing up bubbles and bringing up a boil,
The swamp thing wrapped me in its deadly coil.

"Burble, gasp, burble, cough, burble, burble, choke—"
Those were the very last words that I spoke.
Goodbye, cruel world.

# # #

THE COOKS

Peggy Insula

On a black and moonless night
Two witches stirred a boiling pot
That sent up wisps of sizzling steam
In the hot fire's flickering light.

The green witch growled, "This needs more newt,"
As she took a toothy sip.
The blue witch took a sip herself
And stood a scowling moment mute.

At last, she shook her head and spat.
"No, what this needs is willow root,
Grown close by a fresh-dug grave
Within flight to a cave of bat."

The first witch muttered, "You go there.
It's your turn to harvest that.
Then from a mangy possum's tail
Find us a hollow, greasy hair.

"And for the makings of our stew,
Bring toenail clippings from a bear."
The witches stirred their pot and howled
Around the fire the whole night through.

# # #

THE CRAVEN

Peggy Insula

Once upon a beery teary, while I tripped, drunk and bleary
Over many a sad and empty bottle on the floor —
While I bumbled, nearly hurling, suddenly, a screaming —
Was it a siren, or was I dreaming?
Then came the banging, banging at my trailer door.
That's what it was, and then came more.

Now, I wish I could remember, was it in dire December;
Each shattered Bud Lite spewed its shards upon the floor.
Lord, I wished for my sponsor, who I'd chosen to ignore —
For the wise and patient man whom the drunks call Igor —
Only he ain't here no more.

The heavy, harsh, metallic clatter of my chain lock's snap
Scared me — bared me of excuses futile claimed before;
Now, there came reeking — my bladder, full and leaking,
Leaking on my chamber floor,
"Oh Lord," I cried. "Can there be more?"

With a strange surge of bravado, courage from the bottles,
I proclaim, "Come in, come in, and bring your shackles;
For surely now, you've raised my hackles.
And with the grace God grants to drunkards,
I'm ready for a stinking stay in your dingy dank tank."
Quoth the copper, "That's fer shore."

# # #

A SERIOUSLY SCARY STORY

Betty Whitaker Jackson

I've never loved goblins, or skeletons, or ghosts
And shun the bold supernatural
I hate the whodunits, the mysteries, the cults
And killings, and terror, and such.

There's something in my heart,
I don't know quite what,
But I've lived long enough to embrace it,
I'm sort of a Pollyanna at heart
Loving beauty, and joy and goodness.

I thrive on stories of folks helping others
To make this life more easy
And shed ourselves from all disagreements
And learn mercy and kindness, and love.

The world word be better if everyone changed
From negatives to positive thinking.
Some think it would be boring without some vice
And surprises, and shock, and war's conflicts.

They think we thrive on "dog eat dog,"
And striving to hurt and bury others
In rising to prominence, in getting the goods
On others, defeating and beating them.

Part II: Seriously Scary Stanzas

I'd rather sip my glass of iced tea
And write positive novels
And stories where triumph consists of one thing:
Improving the lifestyles of others.

I know I'm minority, but I raised moral kids
And never dreamed they'd wander
Into drugs, or violence, or demons, occult
To mess up their sensitive psyches.

No guidance counselor visits, no midnight calls
From jail cells or drug dens or taverns,
No Halloween glorying in devils or witches
No curses, no put downs, no dark garbs.

Thrill seekers, find a new path to tread,
Lift folks up, don't push them down,
Love each other by encouraging achievement
Avoid personal scary stories.

# # #

COVID-19

Tim Janecke

Thrust upon us
Unaware of its source
Hurtful and lethal
It moves with great force

Politicians say plenty
News anchors too
Yet people are dying
What do we do?

The doctors and others
Attack this disease
We look for successes
A cure we ask... please

# # #

HALLOWEEN HORRORS

Richard Marschall

We sit on our couches, fearing the worst -
It's Halloween Night, and it's deep, dark, and gray!
Outside our windows, there are goblins and ghosts –
things in the night, little things, that are cursed!

Horrible forms, watching our every move –
macabre and twisted specters, in the dark of night,
moaning, and groaning, and saying: "trick or treat"!
We got the candies - we pray they'll approve!

Phantoms in the night, hideous and pale,
we cringe, and we fain fake fright at our door!
It's the night of the Celts, the dead, at play –
these monsters, these witches - mayhem will prevail!

Their giggles and laughter, do nothing to hide,
the gloaming and the shadows, this world of pretend!
There is no running out of candy, this night of nights-
of Frankenstein, the Lizard Man, and Dracula's bride!

Horrible forms all, to test our resolve!
Crimson splotches, to make it the more real,
unleashed powers, the likes we've never seen,
psychotic images, that seem to evolve!

Ancient grim reminders of holidays past,
sidewalk pumpkins alighting, walkways and yards.

Part II: Seriously Scary Stanzas

Mystical magic – will it never end?
The neighborhood curfew – it's already passed!

Still, stragglers keep rapping at our door,
the little ones now home, with their treasure in tow!
Delightful teens now show up, in their guises of gore,
now out of treats, I think we're in, for Halloween war!

But night passes quickly, the streets are soon cleared.
Evening returns to quiet, and we go to bed,
dreams of a quieter time, and the days ahead,
Halloween horrors, nowhere as bad, as we feared!

# # #

THE NIGHTMARE OF CANCER

Ashley McGrath

Public speaking, spiders, and snakes –
A few things that give people the shakes.
What's really scary is a cancer diagnosis,
Especially when it comes with a bad prognosis.

Sadly, not everyone survives.
Cancer prematurely ends lives.
The fear of an early death
Quickly takes away one's breath.

# # #

HALLOWEEN GUEST

Linda Paul

And so it was last Halloween
A dark and stormy night
No little trick or treaters knock
Only ones with greater height

I sat in my slovenly costume
Candy bowl in my lap
When knocking, knocking at my door
As loud as a thunderclap

Or was it thunder? I decided yes
And stayed put in my chair
I ate another chocolate, then
A great shriek filled the air

No, it wasn't the TV
It was just outside my door
I thought it might have been the cat
Till the knocking resumed once more

I knew I had to answer it
The candy bowl held forward
To distract a sweet-toothed monster
I was shaking like a coward

When the door I opened
Holding out my treats to share

Part II: Seriously Scary Stanzas

"Trick or Drink!" my best friend bellowed
And his laughter filled the air.

#

Precious Publishing Academy – November 5, 2022

1:00pm - 3:00pm at FIT Alumni Center in Melbourne, FL

Technology, the Art of Writing, and the Business of Publishing

Precious Publishing
www.PreciousPublishing.biz

Academy

Anthology Alliance

CTS Press

- Courses
- Webinars
- Workshops

Poetry – Gratitude

The Oxford dictionary defines **gratitude** as "the quality of being thankful; readiness to show appreciation for and to return kindness." As Thanksgiving approaches, our poetry series continues in November with a focus on expressing gratitude for all the good things in our lives – and there are probably more than you think. By adopting an "attitude of gratitude," you can quickly change your perspective. Instead of complaining when the barista doesn't make your coffee exactly the way you want, think of the people going hungry right now in your community. Instead of worrying about how old you are, think about how much better it is than the alternative. Et c'est gratuite.

***

Scott Tilley is president and founder of Precious Publishing, an emeritus professor at the Florida Institute of Technology, president and founder of the Center for Technology & Society, president and co-founder of Big Data Florida, Senior Fellow at the American Security Council Foundation, past president of INCOSE Space Coast, and a Space Coast Writers' Guild Fellow. His recent books include *AFTERMATH* (2022), *PETS* (2021), and *PANDEMIC* (2020). He holds a Ph.D. in computer science from the University of Victoria.

www.PreciousPublishing.biz/join

SHOW ME

Christopher Robin Adams

Show me the scruffy guy crossing against the light,
his broken "need food" cardboard sign
close to his side.
Joan Baez called to mind,
        singing of the unfortunate,
the miserable who waste away
        in poverty's jails,
        in uneducated wastelands,
        in medicine's cruel-twist poor house.
She picked up the songs
        of Seeger,
and he picked up the Dickensonian series,
        the Hugo documents of suffering.
They picked up Saint Francis
and further back to the Jesus guy:
        we can feed all,
        and we can clothe all,
        and we can fix housing, too.
Instead, like Pharoah,
        we prefer to spend
one more night with the frogs
and from our air-conditioned cars,
our leather-covered seats,
        watch the scruffy guy crossing against the light.

# # #

GRATITUDE

Betty Whitaker Jackson

"Thank you, Mommy," my daughter uttered
As I handed her ice cream today.
"What nice manners," the storeowner muttered
As the tot licked the drips away.

Did she thank me later for giving advice,
Or for college tuition or car keys?
Did she thank me for meals, or her latest device
Or giving her a life as she pleased?

Indirectly, I think, when she credited Mom
At graduation as she spoke before crowds,
She thanked us for guidance and buckets of wisdom
She thinks led to honors right now.

On her wedding day, all veiled and so pretty
She, tears in her eyes, held me oh, so tight
Confessing she wanted to emulate me
As she started her family's life.

When we think "Thanks, Mom" in a momentary toss,
It fades into vapor so fast.
But it's foundational truth is never lost,
The gratitude attitude lasts.

# # #

MONEY

Nick Kaplan

"You know that guy at table four."
"Yea, the one that was so funny."

"He wrote me a poem, with wonderful words,"
"But I'd rather have had the money."

# # #

SPACESUIT

Nick Kaplan

In silence vast, space whispers none,
Earthly comforts, here undone.
No breeze, no warmth, just void's embrace.

Across the stars, our journey's traced,
In suits we float, through endless space,
Planets afar, our silent chase.

A mishap strikes, a scent, a swell,
Inside my suit, not all is well,
With AI's fix, in space, I dwell.

# # #

WHAT IS THANKSGIVING?

Richard Marschall

"What is Thanksgiving?" the little one asked.
"Why, it's a time to be thankful for all that we've got,
a time to rejoice, and be of good cheer,
knowing well our deeds, are never for naught!"

"Is it like the time when we took grandma for lunch,
she bought us dessert, after we finished our meal?"
"Yes, my dear, that's exactly what I'm trying to say –
it's the very basic, fundamental, idea of the deal!"

Blessings of a love,
both boundless and infinite,
from the far corners of the universe,
close, personal, noble, and imminent.

"Mother!" the five-year-old inquired that day.
"I've too many toys, for which, I no longer have use!
Can I not give some to others less fortunate than I?
There's my Barbie, my Raggedy Ann, my caboose."

"Why Jennifer, what a marvelous idea!
I'm so proud to say that you are a daughter of mine!
To part with your treasures is so selfless and pure –
for one of your age, I think your plan is divine!"

Blessings of a love,
both boundless and infinite,

Part III: Gratitude

from the far corners of the universe,
close, personal, noble, and imminent.

# # #

THE RIGHT ATTITUDE

Ashley McGrath

If you have a negative attitude,
You should try practicing gratitude.
You might think you don't have enough.
You probably have too much stuff.

It is natural for people to want more.
Remember you're better than you were before.
Your mind should be occupied
With what makes you satisfied.

# # #

BEING ALIVE

Noel Sinchak

Alive I stand, in gratitude and awe,
Of life's close calls and the mysteries I saw.
As a youth, to the skies, my heart took flight,
A thirst to soar, in the day and night.

In Mr. Deptula, my ninth-grade guide,
A pilot of the World War, at his side.
His stories of war, of air, and flight,
Stoked my dreams, in the silent night.

In his words, a path did unfold,
To the Civil Air Patrol, brave and bold.
Search and rescue, our mission's call,
An observer's wings, I earned through all.

To the heavens, I yearned to climb,
In a Piper J-3, in the sky's own time.
Eleven miles I'd ride, under starlit cover,
For each precious hour, above the world to hover.

To Morrisville Airport, my journey led,
In a flight school's shadow, my dreams were fed.
A "line boy" I became, fueling planes, checking oil,
Through long summer days, in the sun's hot toil.

A dance with danger, as propellers roared,
A memory imprinted, forever stored.

Part III: Gratitude

A full throttle start, a close call,
A propeller's dance, a breathless stall.

Experiences gathered, with pilots wide and far,
In skies serene, under moon and star.
One incident, a touch and go landing,
Brought a scare, and harsh reprimanding.

The propeller bent, vibrations raw,
Yet we landed safely, in life's great maw.
Lucky once again, I must confess,
In the arms of the sky, in its vast caress.

* * *

In another tale of skyward roam,
A pilot sought to loop the dome.
With a dive for speed, a pull for height,
But something was amiss in flight.

Straight we plummeted, ground drew near,
The airspeed dial stirred my fear.
Past the red line, we raced on,
A dance with fate, from dusk till dawn.

Five, then ten, then twenty past,
How long would this wild ride last?
The Earth above, in my view,
The world turned askew, as fear grew.

The pilot's error, soon perceived,
Throttle pulled back, we both breathed.
Speed reduced, normal flight resumed,

Part III: Gratitude

In relief, life's joy bloomed.

My private pilot's license, at last, I claimed,
Passengers to the skies, I tamed.
Before the driver's seat was mine,
I had danced with clouds, in the divine.

* * *

Once, I dreamt of fighter flight,
To join the Marines in their skyward fight.
With two years' learning, tests, and check,
The aviation cadet path I chose to trek.

I passed the tests, both bold and stern,
To Willow Grove, I did sojourn.
But alas, my dream, it stumbled and fell,
For my left eye, it did not tell.

The full tale of a fighter's sight,
One eye was perfect, the other slight.
"Blind," they said, "come back when you see,"
My dream of flight, it could not be.

I enlisted in the Air Force blue,
To be near planes, I still wanted to.
Supply, they said, no wings for me,
From Texas to Tampa, then Germany.

At MacDill base, I studied by night,
Gathered credits with scholarly might.
I flew light planes, hitchhiked by day,
Uniformed and young, I found my way.

Part III: Gratitude

Hitchhiked between Tampa and the Sarasota land,
A uniformed thumb, an open hand.
Once, with a trucker on route three-oh-one,
A trip I'll not forget, under Florida's sun.

I warned him of a deadly bend,
But my words he seemed not to comprehend.
Cars pulled aside as we crossed the line,
An impending doom, a silent sign.

He sat in trance, a sleepless sleep,
Into danger's path, we began to creep.
I shouted, I nudged, he awoke with a start,
A tragedy averted, by luck or art.

From that day forth, I've not set foot,
Inside a truck, nor tractor's boot.
The memory lingers, vivid and raw,
Of the day I cheated fate's cruel law.

* * *

In the heartland of Germany, I was stationed,
In aircraft and autos, I roamed, unrationed.
A pilgrimage beckoned in Lourdes, France,
A military gathering, not left to chance.

Four of us journeyed in two cars,
Across the lands, under the stars.
Friendship blossomed, assistance shared,
Each for the other, we truly cared.

Part III: Gratitude

Forty thousand souls in Lourdes, we met,
From NATO nations, no anger or fret.
In unity we prayed, in peace, we smiled,
In that holy town, we were beguiled.

Then Barcelona was our call,
Before returning to Germany's hall.
One car I steered, downhill we raced,
When my brakes faltered, heart fiercely paced.

No hope to slow, speed surged like a tide,
Both lanes blocked, no place to hide.
A critical situation, but then I dared,
To swerve to the right, a collision spared.

On two wheels, we narrowly passed,
Each halted vehicle, breath held fast.
A culvert loomed, concrete and stark,
Again I swerved, in the dimming dark.

The car balanced left, the culvert missed,
Through a vacant field, we coiled and hissed.
Camping gear sprung, an unruly dance,
At last, we halted, given a chance.

Friends circled back, to our aid they sped,
Guided us to a garage, where troubles were shed.
Repair was cheap, but nerves were raw,
In a local eatery, we sat in awe.

A bottle of wine, in minutes drained,
My buddy took the wheel, as I refrained.

Part III: Gratitude

The journey resumed, a steady beat,
No further incident, the trip complete.

* * *

From the U.S. Air Force, I retired in sixty-five,
Postal Service beckoned, for five months, I'd thrive.
Before academia called, my mind's long-lost friend,
In Trenton, as a substitute teacher, my days I'd spend.

At Rutgers University, I take night classes,
In New Brunswick, NJ, amongst the student masses.
A commute of twenty-five miles, Trenton and back,
A journey of knowledge, on a scholarly track.

One night, on US1, divided by concrete grand,
A highway of four lanes, a barrier on either hand.
Tractor trailer to my right, an unwelcome sight ahead,
Headlights on collision course, my heart with dread.

I dared not blink my lights, fear, confusion took hold,
Barrier to my left, trailer on my right, future untold.
An incoming vehicle, speed high, time running thin,
A three-way confrontation, I dreaded to begin.

A moment of luck, as the trailer driver slowed,
Allowed space to move, as the incoming car showed.
What fate met the driver or others in our wake,
I do not know, but good fortune, I hope they'd take.

A memory surfaced, of a time five or six years past,
In Florida, I'd woken a sleeping driver, holding fast.
A sense of gratitude surged, a respect newly earned,

Part III: Gratitude

For the tractor-trailer drivers, a lesson well learned.

* * *

With a B.A. from Rutgers, my academic tale,
I use my G.I. Bill, for flight training without fail.
A commercial pilot's license, a grand scheme,
The U.S. government footed 90%, like a dream.

The program allowed for thrills, aerobatic training,
Hours of defying gravity, my passion sustaining.
Flying wasn't without trials, as one day would show,
A year into training, my courage I had to stow.

A radio signal to New York, a passenger by my side,
Aircraft ahead, an airborne collision seemed to bide.
Flight manual declares, in predicament quite stern,
Both pilots must veer right, a crucial rule to learn.

I executed the move, banking on the other's recall,
Praying he'd also turn right, avoiding a deadly fall.
We mirrored the move, wings vertical to the ground,
A close call once again, but safely, we were found.

* * *

While at college, as a substitute teacher, I toiled,
In Trenton, New Jersey's schools, my life unspoiled.
Through university and beyond, teaching is my route,
The seed of knowledge, in young minds, to sprout.

Furthering my skills, in additional courses I enrolled,
Secondary school teacher, certificate would uphold.

Part III: Gratitude

A journey that led me to a junior high school stage,
Teaching seventh grade social studies, I came of age.

A ninth grade history course, I was also bestowed,
A crucial journey through time, stories to be told.
A challenging task, administrators watchful gaze,
Hustling in urban school districts, I spent those days.

* * *

May of '76, the U.S. Air Force Reserve beckoned me,
Not knowing, this decision would shape my destiny.
The next twenty-five years, a journey across the globe,
To locations unimagined, this path began to probe.

Medical administrative specialist, I first did enlist,
With the 72nd aeromedical evacuation, in its midst.
At McGuire AFB in New Jersey, I found my start,
Cross-trained as loadmaster, a role that's truly an art.

The Lockheed C-141, a four-engine jet, was my ride,
702nd military airlift squadron, my pride.
Loading and offloading cargo, flying in the sky,
Taking care of passengers, always with an eagle eye.

On international flights, paperwork to abide,
Ensuring weight and balance, lest a crash coincide.
Two schools and six months training in flight,
A loadmaster qualification, earned with all my might.

Across America and abroad, missions did I lead,
But Cairo, my heart's yearning, its call I heeded.
Fascinated by pyramids and tales of Egypt's glory,

Part III: Gratitude

I craved to visit, to witness firsthand, pharaoh's story.

A mission, Bright Star, the path to my dream's design,
Held every year in Cairo, it was Egypt's sign.
False start before, waiting in Frankfurt, Germany,
Next year, dream realized, a journey through history.

Seven days in Cairo, missions local, I did charter,
Then to Lages Air Base, my journey became harder.
Ground control personnel, our final mission to ferry,
To U.S.A., from Cairo, their equipment we did carry.

The airport, an abyss of darkness, a crash last year,
The loss of 21 lives, a tragedy severe.
As loadmaster, I promised the anxious crew,
To fit in as much as possible, a promise I'd pursue.

We took off from Cairo, flying high and steady,
Over the Atlantic, for Lages AB, we were ready.
A final inspection before landing, all seemed just fine,
But climbing over a generator, fate crossed the line.

Blood filled my boot, a sharp rip, I was aware,
An ugly wound gashed open, pain hard to bear.
Quick actions by crew, a tourniquet applied,
Safe landing in Lages AB, to hospital I was supplied.

Three stitches inside, and nineteen on the outer skin,
Three days in hospital, medical leave to begin.
The excellent medical care, in time, was my boon,
I returned to teaching, under the winter moon.

* * *

Part III: Gratitude

Amidst my convalescence, an opportunity took flight,
Interview at Willow Grove Air Reserve, within sight.
A federal civil service position, indeed a worthy goal,
With U.S. Air Force Reserve, a training role.

Superintendent of a mobile aerial squadron, my aim,
Supporting air drop mission, in the Reserve's name.
A challenging task, a broad spectrum to steer,
Load, unload, set drop zone, a career to revere.

A month later, my leg healed and strength reclaimed,
Back to full flight status, as the Air Force named.
This healing, crucial for my future aspiration,
The Air Force Reserve required an examination.

Accepted for the job, it was a milestone to revere,
Charting career for 20 years, my path became clear.
From Maryland to Florida, I decided to move,
Selling my house, just suitcases, a journey to improve.

A military hop to Germany, to meet with friends,
To Dover AFB in my car, a trip that transcends.
Outdoor aviary in Ramstein AB, incident unforeseen,
Something in my eye, the sensation was quite keen.

The unease persisted, to the military hospital, I drove,
The oculist's exam, a detached retina it showed.
Without facilities, to a German hospital, I was sent,
University of Saarland, urgent treatment, I was meant.

Arrived, 5000 euros, the hospital demanded,
BC/BS insurance, and military contract commanded.

Part III: Gratitude

They relented, I admitted, under surgeon's steady hand,
A retina reattached, a rubber buckle, a solution grand.

Ten days in hospital, with friends, weeks of recuperation,
Registered outpatient at Ramstein, for regular observation.
Unable to fly until the gas in my eye reduced,
60 days in Germany, before the journey was induced.

Upon reaching Florida, my journey felt just right,
Yet, the driver's eye test brought about a plight.
The detached retina operation, a cataract in its wake,
My sight now compromised, my license at stake.

"A temporary condition," they suggested it might be,
A letter from my doctor, a license granted temporarily.
With the doctor's affirmation, the operation I underwent,
A renewed vision, a path forward, a course now set.

For twenty-one years, a ritual became,
Checkups every six months, in the healing game.
Each appointment a victory, success in every chart,
A testament of resilience, a journey of the heart.

* * *

Seven years past, the end of summer brought a trial,
A lump as big as a golf ball, a moment of denial.
Off to my family doctor, whose concern mirrored mine,
A surgeon's consult he arranged, a signal divine.

The surgeon unsure, but certain of one detail,
The lump had to go, the surgery could not fail.
I agreed and the operation was a swift affair,

Part III: Gratitude

The tissue removed, sent to labs with care.

The local pathologists puzzled, their report unclear,
Sent the sample to Shands Hospital, hoping to endear.
The experts there were decisive, their findings rather stark,
Cancerous cells detected, a journey was about to embark.

A meeting with Dr. Gibbs, chief surgeon of acclaim,
A reassuring tone, as he explained the game.
If one had to have cancer, this was the kind to bear,
Slow in growth, localized, its spread very rare.

But still it had to be excised, the tumor, its cradle, and all,
Every remnant of this foreign body, great and small.
The operation was scheduled, amidst many tests,
A journey to Gainesville, seeking the best.

The surgery was successful, a victory well fought,
Followed by radiation, five weeks of tumultuous thought.
The pattern then emerged, CAT scan every four months,
Watching closely for resurgence, every sign and hunch.

For three years, this was routine, then six months for two,
And yearly scans thereafter, under careful review.
So far, all successful, standing strong in this race,
With every victory, I embrace a new grace.

* * *

In the grand finale of my tale, my heart yearns to confess,
My survival through trials, is not mere chance or guess.
Exponentially exceeded, the close brushes with fate,
I owe it not to luck, but a guardian who's great.

Part III: Gratitude

Yes, I firmly believe, in a higher power's gaze,
A holy spirit's guidance, through life's bewildering maze.
It cradles me in its hands, through the tempest and fray,
Enabling my journey, shaping my way.

Its benevolent shield, preserving my existence,
With an unwavering commitment, offering consistent assistance.
Every breath I take, every new dawn I see,
I thank these divine forces, for their grace upon me.

In the orchestration of my life, their song echoes clear,
Each note a blessing, every melody I hold dear.
But it's more than sheer luck, that has brought me this day,
I'm a vessel of divine will, in every single way.

For this, I am thankful, my gratitude knows no bounds,
In the whispers of the wind, in the silence that resounds.
My journey continues, under this holy decree,
To be here with you, the greatest blessing there could be.

~~~

Back to where I began, this reflective narrative of life,
A question loomed large, amid moments of strife.
Why am I still here, when fate has often swung its scythe?
Is there more to contribute, in this grand drama, so rife?

I believe there's an answer, extending my earlier thought,
An uncharted territory, that I must yet have sought.
There must be some purpose, a mission yet unsought,
An achievement, an accomplishment, a battle yet fought.

Part III: Gratitude

A divine design plays out, through chapters of my time,
An unfathomable script, in a language so sublime.
The tapestry of life continues to chime,
Guiding me to a purpose, up the existential climb.

Yes, there's more to my journey, more that I must do,
A path yet to tread, a sightline to pursue.
For every sunrise paints the sky anew,
Each day, an opportunity to continue my life's review.

# # #

Precious Publishing Academy – December 3, 2022

1:00pm - 3:00pm at FIT Alumni Center in Melbourne, FL

Technology, the Art of Writing, and the Business of Publishing

Precious Publishing
www.PreciousPublishing.biz

Academy

Anthology Alliance   CTS Press

- Courses
- Webinars
- Workshops

Poetry – Happy Holidays

Perry Como's 1954 recording of "There's No Place Like Home for the Holidays" is a perennial favorite, reflecting our deep-seated urge to return to a simpler time during the hectic holiday season. Happy memories of holidays from years ago tend to center on family, friends, and food. Our modern holiday season reaches its feverish peak with Christmas and Chanukah. Poems celebrating the holidays vary from children's tales to mystical missives. Which is *your* favorite?

'Twas the night before Christmas, when all through the house Not a creature was stirring, not even a mouse; The stockings were hung by the chimney with care, In hopes that St. Nicholas soon would be there; The children were nestled all snug in their beds, While visions of sugar-plums danced in their heads;	
From *A Visit from St. Nicholas* (1844)	Clement Clarke Moore (1779-1863)

***

Scott Tilley is president and founder of Precious Publishing, an emeritus professor at the Florida Institute of Technology, president and founder of the Center for Technology & Society, president and co-founder of Big Data Florida, Senior Fellow at the American Security Council Foundation, past president of INCOSE Space Coast, and a Space Coast Writers' Guild Fellow. His recent books include *AFTERMATH* (2022), *PETS* (2021), and *PANDEMIC* (2020). He holds a Ph.D. in computer science from the University of Victoria.

www.PreciousPublishing.biz/join

HILLBILLY CHRISTMAS

Peggy Insula

Christmas Eve was finally here.
Paw stretched out by the stove and slurped on a beer.
Granny came in and shot him a glare.
The hound at Paw's feet cringed at her stare.
Hands on her hips, Granny told the old coot,
"It's Jesus's birthday, you drunken galoot!
Show a little respect for this holy night,
Or I'll give you a real jolly Christmas Eve fight!
You should fall on your knees and give thanks to God
For letting you live one more year, you great clod!"

# # #

YUM!

Peggy Insula

"Gobble, gobble, gobble,"
Were the last words he said
Before Granny crammed him full
of stuffing made of bits of bread,
Celery, nuts, and apple slices
Lib'rally laced with wine
And yummy sage and other spices
To create a taste so fine
Along with the gravy from the drippin's
In the aromatic pan
Where the turkey stood a-sizzlin'.

To the table we all ran
While salivating from inhaling
The rich, turkey basted air.
"We've waited all year long
For this luscious feast to share,"
We spluttered as we stuttered,
And "Gobble, gobble, gobble"
Were the last sounds we uttered.

# # #

HOLIDAYS ARE NOT ALWAYS HAPPY

Betty Whitaker Jackson

With his uncreased pillow and empty chairs,
My longing heart is breaking
To think I'll ne'er share holidays' joys
With my lover's now-vacant presence
Distresses.

The card, embossed, signed "All My Love"
And his fluent scrawl –"Me," I'll treasure,
The gift unopened, from hints subtly dropped
(All I need is his presence)
No presents.

Now, He'd tell me, with serene sincerity,
To nevermore fret, not to worry.
"I'm content and waiting 'til Somewhen, My Dear,
Like before we were married, remember?"
Patient endurance.

I'll resurrect those feelings, the embraces, the kisses
In memories so hauntingly reminiscent.
How we hated to part then, and now so much worse
Our togetherness bond is now severed.
Alone in solitude.

Part IV: Happy Holidays

How to spend holidays, feeling so depressed?
Look to our legacy's celebration
Nonchalantly today, they're creating the splendor
They'll long lifetimes hopefully treasure
Tender togetherness.

Let us capture the energy, hold longer the embraces
And put to rest moments that shatter
The fragility of mortality, the inevitable pattern
Of generations passing forever —
Opportunities, irretrievable

When nonchalant holidays pass year after year,
Never imagining we'd face the divide
So deep, so disparate, so lonely, so desperate,
Sometimes it doesn't seem real.
Unfathomable separation.

To wish he were here, with the mortal ills present
Would be a selfish impediment,
I'll have holidays and holy days and long nights alone
But have our memories to soothe me
Faint comfort.

But finally, working through the stages of grief,
I'll find dispassionate acceptance
And know that my days are in God's loving care,
Will others mourn, noting my passing?
Or notice.

The curse of Adam and Eve persists still,
the ultimate battle we face,

Part IV: Happy Holidays

Death, where is thy sting? Grave, thy victory?
In Christ only I stand
Resurrected.

The clouds of witnesses who have supported me well
Assuring me that death is earth's passage
To eternal worship of God Who created
Caring hearts to love and to mourn—
Redemption, the true holiday.

# # #

This is NOT a true experience. My husband and I have been happily married for over fifty years and treasure every day we're together. But for many of our octogenarian friends, holidays are no longer happy.

ENCHANTMENT

Richard Marshall

E very moment of our lives entirely blessed

N oel we sing to the angels on high

C aptivated by the creation of man on this Earth

H umbled by the meaning of our Lord's Work Devine

A ttracted by the lights, the colors, and sounds

N ativity reminds us the cause, this glorious occasion

T hrilled to be a part of this enlightenment unbound

M onopolized by the clarity of His Message supreme

E nraptured in the elegance of all of God's Signs

N ascency of a new day of the Alpha and Birth

T urned by Jesus' Message - Love, Hope, and Charity

# # #

THE CELEBRATION OF HOLIDAYS

Ashley McGrath

The end of the year includes holidays.
We all look forward to these special days.
Parties, tasty food, and gifts
Give us emotional lifts.

Our holiday traditions vary.
They're a break from the ordinary.
Regardless of how we celebrate,
Holidays put us in a joyful state.

# # #

CHRISTMAS NIGHT

Darci Wolcott

We were quiet coming home
Pensive, a bit nostalgic even then

Hurtling down the dark highway
Kids asleep in the back seat
hugging their new toys, their little hands
sticky with candy-canes
Bellies full of tradition,
sated and satisfied

The dashboard lights and occasional
flash from the brights of a passing car
played the last illuminations of the season
on the long ride back from the
home where my husband grew up

They had waved good-bye from their front porch
Two smiling white-haired figures
straight out of a Hallmark movie
perhaps indulging memories of their own
Now it's our turn to wave – 'love you,
drive safely, thanks for coming' –
It went so fast!

Through the telescope of time
We remember those we lost
Those we honored, those we raised

Part IV: Happy Holidays

Those we still embrace

Full of memories – laughter, tears
We're grateful for the fullness of our years.

# # #

Precious Publishing Academy – February 4, 2023
1:00pm - 3:00pm at the West Melbourne Public Library

Technology, the Art of Writing, and the Business of Publishing

Precious Publishing
www.PreciousPublishing.biz

Academy

Anthology Alliance
CTS Press

• Courses   • Webinars   • Workshops

Poetry – Love & Compassion

And though the rich buy power for a time / One thing that money can't buy / Love and compassion
And though I know it's gonna take some time / Someday we're all gonna find / Love and compassion

"Love and Compassion" from *Small Victories* by The Parachute Club (1986)

Valentine's Day is perhaps the ultimate poetic holiday, full of themes of love and compassion. Ode poems are replete with romantic celebrations of people, places, or events. Which is *your* favorite? What does love mean to you? Affection? Broken hearts? Compassion? Empathy? Sympathy?

***

Scott Tilley is president of Precious Publishing, an emeritus professor at the Florida Institute of Technology, president of the Center for Technology & Society, president and co-founder of Big Data Florida, president of the Space Coast Progressive Alliance, a member of the Florida Writers Association Board of Directors, and a Space Coast Writers' Guild Fellow. His recent books include *AFTERMATH* (2022), *PETS* (2021), *Systems Analysis & Design* (2020), and *Technical Justice* (2019). He holds a Ph.D. in computer science from the University of Victoria.

www.PreciousPublishing.biz/join

THE COMPARISON

Christopher Robin Adams

Friendship is a peanut butter sandwich:
it's nourishing and consistent.
We all know what to expect:
its creaminess for our mouth,
its periodic crunch between teeth
or utter smoothness over tongue and gum,
its choking attention-getting
     if disrespected
       and eaten too fast.
We know this.

Love is not a peanut butter sandwich.
Love is a truffle chocolate.
Unbalanced, it provides fuel,
near-predigested near-perfect near-pure carbs.
It urges the faster talk,
gases the quicker walk;
it brings out puns uncalled for
and pushes against the closed door.
It releases ahhhhhhs and hmmmmmms
and spikes energy until endorphins enter;
then, pains are forgotten,
and we are one more step
     from the reality we know
      and the cliff just beyond the blueberries.

Part V: Love & Compassion

Friendship may move toward love,
but it will be a blended kind,
a peanut butter cup flavor.
It may have heat,
but not the same white-heat
of pure chocolate-truffle love.

The risk of the latter
– always –
is what to do in a carb-crash.
Ideally, if any sense remains,
one reaches for the peanut butter cup
just to keep living,
but settles for a peanut butter sandwich.

You know what I mean.
You know it:
"Can we remain friends?"

Yes … and no.

Yes, if you can relax on a couch
with a peanut butter sandwich,
savoring the knowledge
that this is a very healthy meal
and that it will get you through the day
and nourish you through the night,
carry you through the rest of the week
and beyond.

No, if you cannot forget.
If you cannot forget the bike rides with wind blowing
through hair,

songs erupting in the middle of Costco.
No, if you cannot turn loose of roofs disappearing
and blue sky and billowy clouds above.
No, if you cannot abandon the shaking earth,
if you cannot accept the emotional tumult erupting
midday
when a tear moistens your eye
and a friend asks,
"Are you ok?"

Think about it.

If you understand the comparison,
you're ready for February;
if you do not,
watch yourself,
buckle your seat belt,
and hang on for dear life.

# # #

WHAT ARE YOU TO ME?

Peggy Ball

You're the reason for this rhyme,
You're the loving ties that bind;

You're the music for my dance;
You're the thrill of my romance.

On my bracelet you're a charm;
On cold nights you keep me warm.

You're the chiming of a bell;
You're my wishes in a well.

You're the apples in my pie;
You're my hanky when I cry.

You're the oysters in my stew;
You're my pep talk when I'm blue.

You're the lolly in my pop;
You're my love that doesn't stop.

You are everything that's fine,
And the best part is YOU'RE MINE!

# # #

Eugenio

Peggy Insula

I hope they bury us together.
I can't sleep not snuggled up to you.
I synchronize my breath with yours,
Your strength and warmth imbue.

You are the rock I lean on —
Steadfast, sure, and true.
Your firm support fails never —
I'm so in love with you.

Your warm brown eyes reflect your love;
You broadcast masculinity.
You shelter me from all life's storms —
I'm yours for all eternity.

Te quiero.

# # #

LOVE AND COMPASSION

Betty Whitaker Jackson

I always ran my classroom
As a place to be safe and authentic
To listen to all, consider all sides,
And respect each other's opinions.

My students could celebrate
Their personal victories,
And treat others with compassion
Who struggled to learn or conform.

With mutual celebration
We found miniscule and major victories
When everybody learned
And everyone therefore earned

We found true camaraderie.
Students aiding each other's learning.
To study, explore, and create
Was better than critique and eviscerate,

When they decided to cooperate.
They loved to read others' pieces
And first find the points to elevate,
Then, if needed, to expand.

The sting became encouragement.
We still maintain stringent standards

Part V: Love & Compassion

And strove for excellent achievement
That made it a true celebration

When our scores, together, soared.
They say rising tide lifts all ships.
In my classrooms, we proved it,
With love and compassion, it worked.

# # #

MY PSALM 502 (WEDDING DAY)

Betty Whitaker Jackson

Eternal Father, we pray on this special day
Your blessing on this couple,
Be very real as they pledge their vows
To stay close to them and bless their union.

You who hung the stars in the heavens
You who stop ocean waves on the shore
Yet live in our hearts through Your Holy Spirit
And save our souls through Your Son.
We honor and bless Your Name.

Each year is a gift from You, Dear Lord,
Each breath in Your command,
Each chance encounter, each conversation
Has prepared their hearts for this day.

You knit their bones, their sinews, their smiles,
Gave strength, yet left each one lacking,
Preparing them for each other's completion
Answered prayers to bond them together.
We bless Your Name, and give your praise
Foreknowing this day would on time come
You've guided, protected, cared, and prepared
Them as witness to Your plan.

Part V: Love & Compassion

You've known each one, You've raised them well
So they would come together
You granted talents, and gifts, and souls
To blend them for each other.

Now, going forward, cement their union
As they learn to walk together
Following Your will for their future, Your plan
They'll discover Your revealing when it's time.

Let them never know want or need
When they call on Your faithful providence.
Keep them humble as they pray and seek Your will.
Reflect how You've guided and planned Life well.

And when, so far away now, they're turning grey
And memories are stronger than adventure can bring,
May they cherish this day, this wonderful beginning
When they promised commitment this wedding day.

# # #

Previously published in *Encore: An Anthology of Stories and Poems* (2018) and used here with permission.

GROWING OLD

Tim Janecke

I didn't think I would get old
There were schools and jobs
Parties and girls
It seemed it would last forever

I didn't think I would get old
Time would pass but I would live forever
Forgiveness for others
And to myself

Mistakes and loss
Wins and heights so high
Loss and failures some times
I didn't think I would get old

#

WINGS

Tim Janecke

The power is too great
That's now clear to see
It's time to surrender
It's how it must be

I need help from another
Just whom shall I ask
I need a strong veteran
But who'll take the task

A well-powered spirit
That's what it should be
Include a firm healer
Come here and save me

Liabilities in my past
There's nothing to hide
Sharing all from this catalog
I'm safe now inside

It's time to get ready
These feelings unsure
Anger confusion
Let God be my cure

* * *

Part V: Love & Compassion

Preparing a long list
The people I've harmed
Friends and my family
The hurts I once charmed

To make needed confessions
To most of my friends
And take responsibility
Here now my amends

Emotions upset the day
When balance is the goal
Spot check or long retreats
We do this for our soul

Meditation and close looks
And balance from another
Lift our eyes to the great heights
We belong to God... and each other

# # #

PRAYERS FOR A FRIEND

Richard Marschall

When we're most in need of a helping hand,
when the darkest clouds seem to have their way,
when life, is at its lowest ebb,
our faith reaffirmed, with the *light,* of each new day!

When the waters too wide,
and the mountain too high,
God can make, the waters to part,
and the *heavens,* to shine through the sky!

Yea, even when we are bathed,
in the Stygian darkness, of the pits of hell,
even when our lives seem shrouded,
by death's, ominous knell.

God is there with us.
He stands by our side.
We are *strong,*
with God as our guide!

In that dark valley
of our darkest night,
there is **always** His Beacon,
His Everlasting Light.

And when we're at our lowest ebb
of the depths of our despair,

Part V: Love & Compassion

Christ is always within you,
His Message to share!

The comfort of our Lord,
His compassion and grace,
His life is within us – He is,
our Earthly support, and Holy embrace.

Our cries to our Maker,
our mortal bequests,
our prayers to our God,
for those we hold, most close to our breast!

For it is so written in the ancient scrolls,
and *in*, the Words of our King –
the *promise* to all, that we are *never* alone.
Let it ring! Let it ring!

This prayer to our friend,
wishing you all the very best,
may, God grant you a fast recovery,
and may you *be*, fully blessed!

Our prayers are there for you,
like the arms of the great oak tree,
the blessings of our love -
tis' the *Lord's* guarantee!

#

Written in response to a letter a man received from his best friend, after informing him that he had cancer.

THE MAKINGS OF A BETTER WORLD

Ashley McGrath

Love and compassion
Never go out of fashion.
Mother Teresa's life has inspired
Us to be kind even when we're tired.

Following the Golden Rule
Would make people less cruel.
War and violence would decrease,
Perhaps leading to world peace.

# # #

SHOWER WITH COMPASSION

Carol Schweitzer

Love and compassion are about connecting
And how things feel when we remember:
>How we feel standing, unsupported, alone
>How we help others feel special and grow
>How we give to, and receive, support from others
>How we handle those who mislabel, gossip, abuse
>How we seek anonymity, but sad when abandoned
>How we are Touched, Kissed, Loved, and Cradled.

It's about our God-given moment, an instant chance,
To climb down through someone's side-long glance
Into the center of what they are all about.

The teeniest moment in eternity
Split open, swiftly in then quickly out,
But long enough for us to sneak a peek.
To see the way they really are, down inside.
And when we are there – in that flash – our hearts cry
Seeing the mirror, we want to deny
>Raw hurt
>Confusion
>Joy
>Or vanishing Hope.
We notice the soft sweetness of their sigh
That has shrouded what is so badly longed for
And kept hidden with bravado.

Part V: Love & Compassion

In that second, we find ourselves relating to their strife.
We want to touch their hearts - fend off their hurt from life
That cracks smiles into the corners of their eyes.
We reach, to lift up the down-curve of mouths and minds
That can't try "Fake Happy", their hearts are crying.

Honor this space with them. Give them what they can use
But are too proud or fearful to ask of you.

In this silent, spiritual conversation
We in turn gain new revelation
As we watch our giving bring peace and grace to soar,
Lit by borrowed fire, we ignite again, dignity in their core
Because another heart sat beside, cared, and saw
The tumultuous shaking of their inner wars,
Struggling to stay on the path, praying, Why? What-for?

Let them sense your empathetic spirit buoy,
That stands near, defying all that steals or destroys
Any glory earned from their journey's struggling,
Or prevent their reaching God's given blossoming!

A smile of support makes their hurts seem small,
Pumps up their vigor by a friend, so rare that call
Reminding them they are not victims without leverage
During their private battlefield of courage.

Love and compassion help us change their anger's hot sear
To God's cool wash of get-up-and-go and leaving fear.

# # #

LETTER TO A FRIEND

Noel Sinchak

From a place of deep regret, I pen this letter to you,
My tardiness with these photos, believe me, it's true.
Countless sympathy cards I browsed, none seemed right,
To express my sorrow for your son's unfortunate plight.

Words are often insufficient to capture the ache,
But may these heartfelt lines a difference make.
As you navigate through this devastating wave,
May your friends and kin be your stronghold brave.

One may say, "I know how you feel," a statement untrue,
For each pain is unique, only known to you.
In 2007, I was lost, my grandson's life abruptly ceased,
Tragedy our Florida home, on him, death unfairly feasted.

For weeks, I struggled to sleep, to eat, trapped in despair,
Pepita, my wife, found help, a burden too heavy to bear.
My brother flew in from New Jersey, my sister too,
Their support helped me endure, as I hope it does for you.

* * *

No one can forecast what life holds, the pain or the relief,
My own tale is a testament to that belief.
Back in '81, a near-death brush changed my life's path,
A serious leg cut could've ended my flight, the aftermath.

Part V: Love & Compassion

Had it not healed, Air Force Reserve would not be my fate,
And my civil service career would've never taken shape.
Another episode, in 2002, on a German tour,
A detached retina forced me to endure.

An operation at a German hospital, I had to bide,
Ten days I spent there, until my sight was again allied.
I was grounded for 60 days, unable to fly,
But eventually, I was fit to return to the sky.

Back to the USA, to Palm Bay, I drove my last load,
In a 15-foot truck, my future abode.
The ordeal of one eye healed, my life resumed its pace,
A reminder of how quickly life can change its face.

I am sending you newspaper clippings, consolation words,
In times of loss, they've been comforting chords.
May they bring you and Gail comfort, however small,
In these trying times, as you, Larry, stand tall.

# # #

Precious Publishing Academy – March 4, 2023

1:00pm - 3:00pm at the West Melbourne Public Library

Technology, the Art of Writing, and the Business of Publishing

Precious Publishing
www.PreciousPublishing.biz

Academy

Anthology Alliance

CTS Press

• Courses   • Webinars   • Workshops

Poetry – Spring Forward

It's About Time

"People like us, who believe in physics, know that the distinction between past, present, and future is only a stubbornly persistent illusion."
– Albert Einstein

They say time travel is science fiction, but we spring forward by one hour every year. We cross time zones on airplanes, sometimes arriving before we leave on international flights. If you have a plutonium-powered DeLorean, you can satisfy Huey Lewis' admonishment to "get back in time."

What is *your* favorite time-related poem? Do you like Shakespeare's *Sonnet 19*? T. S. Eliot's *Burnt Norton*? Edgar Allan Poe's *Annabel Lee*? William Blake's *Jerusalem*? Coldplay's *Clocks*?

***

Scott Tilley is president of Precious Publishing, an emeritus professor at the Florida Institute of Technology, president and founder of the Center for Technology & Society, president and co-founder of Big Data Florida, a member of the Florida Writers Association Board of Directors, and a Space Coast Writers' Guild Fellow. His recent books include *AFTERMATH* (2022), *PETS* (2021), *Systems Analysis & Design* (2020), and *Technical Justice* (2019). He holds a Ph.D. in computer science from the University of Victoria.

www.PreciousPublishing.biz/join

It's Time for a Poem

Christopher Robin Adams

I sat down
and thought about time,
the time I spent reading,
the times books opened doors,
the times magazines opened windows.

See, we think of books
as so strong and so powerful;
we ban books and shelve them under counters;
we put them on top shelves
to keep them out of hands.

Magazines slip through the demons,
slide past the burning fingers of 451,
fold up and scuttle into bags,
and roll themselves up and climb into coat pockets.

One such magazine did the latter,
found an unlikely place in my house,
and as I prepared to twiddle thumbs
and pass time by,
I saw it,
opened it,
leafed through it
      until I was snagged
      by "mother-in-law" in a letter.
      It told of a women

who talked to her husband's mother
more than her own mother.
In a warp of time,
brain switches moved from paper to memory.
A second. Less.
I realized I talked to my daughter-in-law
more than my own son.
Then a moment slid by. Less.
I thought of Paul Simon's time slipping away,
Maya Angelou's certain end,
Steve Miller's slipping into the future,
Cat Steven's moon shadow,
and Charles Dickens' letting it eat him away.

I looked at my watch.
A minute later, I glanced at it again.
I reached into my pocket
and gently punched my son's phone number into it.

# # #

INTOXICATING ROSES

Helen Bennett

Intoxicating roses,
Pink, white, red,
Intoxicating roses,
How they go to my head!
They stand among the wildflowers
To symbolize romance,
And just a whiff of roses
Sends me into a trance.

Their fragrance is alluring,
Their petals soft as silk,
Their roundness reassuring
As mothers' milk.
They innocently beckon
And promise to behave,
Until one inhalation
Makes you their slave.
As moments to admire them
Turn into hours,
They let you know why roses
Are queens among flowers.

# # #

THE LAND OF TULIPS AND DAFFODILS

Helen Bennett

I loved to wander among the hills
In the land of tulips and daffodils;
'Twas surely one of my greatest thrills
To hear the earliest robin's trills!

It's the land where leaves turn red and gold
Where trees are a wonder to behold,
Where wandering leaf-watchers abound,
Where nature's bounty is truly found.

It's the land of icicles and chills,
Of skis, and sleds, and toboggan spills,
A land of icy roads and snow,
Where temperatures reach 20 below.

Who needs the tropics where tall palm trees
Flutter their branches in the breeze?
I'm simply bound by memories
To places where I'm bound to freeze!

# # #

THE TULIP OR THE ROSE

Helen Bennett

I prefer the tulip
With its candid little cup;
I prefer the tulip
With its petals pointing up.
Others may admire
The convoluted rose,
Its mysteries and secrets
Never to disclose.
Ponder the enigma
That makes the rose uptight;
Look inside the tulip,
Its stamens stand upright.
Fluted little fellow
Standing straight and tall,
Pink, magenta, yellow,
Fairest flower of all.
Colors so translucent
They can bear no name,
Blending like the sunrise,
Fleeting as a flame.

Rich arrays of roses
Favored by the pen
Far outnumber tulips
In the songs of men.
You will not see tulips
Grace bridal bouquets,

Part VI: Spring Forward

You will not hear poets
Often sing their praise.
Valentines bear roses,
Dearly one must pay
Just to please his sweetheart
With this sweet cliché.

Tulips are majestic
Standing on the mall;
Transient as roses,
Swiftly they must fall.
Why require roses
Just to turn some heads?
I prefer the tulips
In their graceful beds.

Let us reinvent
The symbol of the rose
To stand for faded beauty
Resting in repose.
For the youthful tulip
Gladly we'll make room,
Symbolizing candor
In its fullest bloom.

# # #

TAKING TIME FOR GRANTED

Peggy Insula

Time tromps toward the future,
or is it the past?
The sun outside my window
Was moving pretty fast—
Not up or down, but sideways,
Each move diff'rent from the last.

I knew that God would punish us
For messing with the clocks.
I sat on my bed and wondered
What I was doing with my socks
While outside the geese were flying
Backwards in great flocks.

I stomped into the kitchen
And muttered to myself,
But my coffee had unbrewed
And my cup sat on the shelf.
I scratched my head and searched
But found no wayward elf.

In fear, I opened my front door
To find my morning paper leaving,
Gripped by my faithful paper boy,
His backward footsteps weaving
Down the stairs and to his car
With the sack that he was heaving.

Part VI: Spring Forward

No puzzles here for me today,
Or for me today no puzzles?
I found it harder to think straight;
My head was all abuzzle.
I staggered off to search
For some medicine to guzzle.

The wall clocks had exploded.
They were useless anyhow.
My houseplants shrank to seedlings;
My dog, a puppy now.
Hey! Maybe I was younger!
At the mirror, I yelled, "Wow!"

Humans are adaptable.
Maybe good would come of this.
Could we relive times when we'd messed up?
Change times of sorrow for times of bliss?
I smiled as I anticipated
Reliving my first kiss.

# # #

HERONESQUE BALLET

Betty Whitaker Jackson

Blithe, lightly borne on beveled-winged edges
The gliding white heron heralds pristine pre-dawn,
Smoothly soaring with satiny grace, now
Pirouetting, performing her classic Ballet.

A blur, then a whirr, impressionist's vision
She circles, advances, retreats, 'cross the stage
Artistically, silently, measuring distance, she
Chooses her mark, lands with perfect control.

Poised, precarious, Sur les Pointes, heron wades,
Swirling eddies, glistening rings, on cue, center stage,
At one with the marsh scene, perfection personified
Picturesque, in milieu, blending form, sight, and sound.

Ballerina, au naturale, she ends her performance
Statuesque, silhouetted, awaiting applause,
The marsh grass her audience, the reeds a felled curtain,
Like green willow bending, she bows for bouquets.

# # #

Previously published in *Encore: An Anthology of Stories and Poems* (2018) and used here with permission.

TIME IS OF THE ESSENCE

Richard Marschall

Time my friend, seems to purposefully elude us.
Einstein called it "but a stubborn illusion"!
In his "Cries in the Wilderness" Marschall christens it
"the mother of eternity – contradictory"!
Like the elusive snow leopard, which is seldom seen,
time defies meaning – you can't see it or feel it.
It's the phantom in the opera that no one spies!
We don't know where it begins or if, it has an end!
It traps us in the dark catacombs of our mind,
loosening its rage, as the electric to the storm
In Marschall's "(the) Meaning of Time", he calls it, that
"elusive, indefinable, continuum…"
that mocks our own mortality. It, is the crux
of our sorrows, and the bane, of our corporeal being!
Time is a continuum, a timeline, an event.
Without time there is nothing, no beginning or end!
"Time out! Daytime! Nighttime! Day light savings time!
Move the clock forward! Set it back! Gain time! Lose time!
Hit the alarm! Save time! Do we ever gain time?
Fall is my favorite "time" of the year. "Fall back"
is the mantra heard before the winter solstice!
When our plane flies eastward, we "gain" time, don't we?
It can be 3 pm in Melbourne and 10 in France,
So isn't it earlier and we still have our day?
Not exactly our pilot explains, because no
matter where you are, it's the same time at home. "Huh?"
And Daylight Savings Time, is kind of the same!

Part VI: Spring Forward

You haven't gained a thing when you wake up the next
morn. You haven't gained anything cause everything's
relative, and at some point, you'll have to "Spring ahead",
which puts you back to where you started off in the
first place, six months ago. I don't have a clue, but
like my attorney friend says: "Time is of the essence"!

#

SPRINGING FORWARD

Ashley McGrath

We begrudgingly change our clocks
Before the vernal equinox.
Advancing clocks one hour ahead
Makes it harder to get out of bed.

In this way, time can be manipulated.
This issue has been debated.
Daylight saving time has gotten flak.
We want to get the hour we lost back.

# # #

STEP INTO SPRING

Carol Schweitzer

Open Spring's door and step out of Winter's dark
Into new day's light shining into our heart.
Transcending "What Was" with nature's healing art,
Wiping away strife with hope – a new start.

No longer living life from the outside in,
Instead, shining inside-outward where growth begins.

Divinity's miracle over hibernation season
Awakes from sleep without images or reason.
Peeking out from darker memories that slumber,
Moving on from old lessons too many to number.

Stepping out - not sideways - or backward - but toward,
Spring's trumpeting new lift, her victory's reward.

# # #

ON TIME AND TRAVEL

Noel Sinchak

A DeLorean I have not, like Back to the Future's plot,
Nor a Star Trek transporter, in time's web caught.
Yet time, it seems, has a peculiar way,
Of carrying me forth, and back, in a day.

Hear me out, before you claim me mad,
A tale of journeys, of future and past,
Across time zones, fast and slow,
In the U.S. Air Force Reserve's ebb and flow.

A loadmaster I was, at McGuire AFB,
In the 702nd squadron, o'er land and sea,
Aboard the C-141A/B, a starlifter of might,
Through countless missions, day and night.

From July till August, let me narrate,
A tale of time, and of fate.
McGuire to Keflavik, Iceland's shore,
Cargo exchanged, the bitter cold we bore.

Then to Virginia, Langley AFB,
And onward to Rota, Spain, across the sea.
Athens, Greece, and Nairobi's plain,
In East Africa, as they oft exclaim.

Fire in an engine, we came to face,
Yet we landed safely, in Nairobi's embrace.

Part VI: Spring Forward

Days seven or eight, for a new engine we did wait,
Our venture, held in the hands of fate.

A safari granted, in the final days,
A Tarzan movie scene, in memory stays.
Dancing natives, children in dirt,
Photos aplenty, until the film did hurt.

A taxi ride, a film returned,
A tip for the driver, graciously earned.
From Nairobi to Diego Garcia, we soared,
Mount Kilimanjaro, in the distance roared.

To Athens, Greece, we went once more,
A protest, topless women bore.
Back to Rota, Spain, then Norfolk's shore,
And finally, McGuire AFB, as before.

A few days' rest, then in the air anew,
To Sicily, Italy, and Germany too.
Then Denmark and Massachusetts, a diverse treat,
And back to McGuire, the journey complete.

Forty-four time zones, I'd traveled through,
More than the world's count, it's true.
So, did I travel back in time, you ask,
Or forward, into the future's task?

#

Precious Publishing Academy – April 1, 2023

1:00pm - 3:00pm at the West Melbourne Public Library

Technology, the Art of Writing, and the Business of Publishing

Precious Publishing
www.PreciousPublishing.biz

Academy

Anthology
Alliance

CTS
Press

• Courses   • Webinars   • Workshops

Poetry – Fooled Again

I'll tip my hat to the new Constitution
Take a bow for the new revolution
Smile and grin at the change all around
Pick up my guitar and play
Just like yesterday
Then I'll get on my knees and pray
We don't get fooled again

Won't Get Fooled Again
— Pete Townshend (1971)

Do you fall for April Fool's tricks every year? Even though you know it's coming, do you still find yourself getting punked on April 1? Even though you dutifully follow the maxim to "Beware the Ides of March," do you find yourself falling prey to pranks just two weeks later? If so, don't worry! Just keep calm and carry on, knowing that April Fool's Day has been canceled for 2023.

***

Scott Tilley is president of Precious Publishing, an emeritus professor at the Florida Institute of Technology, president and founder of the Center for Technology & Society, president and co-founder of Big Data Florida, a member of the Florida Writers Association Board of Directors, and a Space Coast Writers' Guild Fellow. His recent books include *AFTERMATH* (2022), *PETS* (2021), *Systems Analysis & Design* (2020), and *Technical Justice* (2019). He holds a Ph.D. in computer science from the University of Victoria.

www.PreciousPublishing.biz/join

THE WRECKAGE OF AN APRIL ONE STORY

Christopher Robin Adams

The teaching position was mine
after an eleven-month search,
but I didn't have the piece of paper
that said I was certified by the state;
it was in the mail, I knew,
but it was in my Post Office Box,
and that I didn't know.
So, skipping the mailbox stop,
I did what children have done for centuries
in times of stress:
I headed home.
Not straight home,
though that was the intention,
but home through a head-on collision
that segued into a helicopter ride
and some surgeries
with stitches, casts, and crutches.
Whose divided attention in whose head
was never decided;
witnesses went back to college
and never appeared in court.
Whatever punishment
for the torn and scabbed bodies
of the five individuals involved
and the loss of two cars

Part VII: Fooled Again

remains in those four other folks' thoughts.

As such, I was left with memories of the wreckage only
because the brain scrubbed
the twelve hours from the vehicles' impact
to the wake-up with mother and brother
looking down at me,
at my bruised, broken, and bandaged body.
Science tells us
the brain tortoises up
and protects itself
from painful memories
of physical and mental trauma.
The only record I have
remains the incident's artifacts:
       a mangled port-wine car,
       a piece of door cut by jaws-of-life
       leveraged by police officers
       as they worked to extract me,
       a rod of titanium removed
       from my snapped-then-healed arm,
       a blood-soaked beige-and-blue beach towel
       that a witness had wrapped
       around my torn-scalp head,
       a police report
       that recorded answers I gave
       while still imprisoned in my crushed car,
       county records that documented
       the helicopter with pilot and paramedic
       that airlifted me to the hospital,
       and hospital records that documented
       the twenty-four individuals and companies

who contributed to my recovery.
My future wife told me
years later
traffic was backed up at least five miles
eastward to the interstate
and her car was locked into that grid,
a memorable note as she missed her dinner-date
that evening.
Missing from the car's remains
was the Bluebird of Happiness
I had epoxied to the dashboard;
with no bits of glass in evidence,
it apparently flew away,
perhaps as it saw the impending crash.

As April Fool's Day arrives again,
again I reflect on that day.
with no emotional trauma from memories,
I just have varieties of directions
for meaning:
I have helped some 3,000 students
learn to clarify ideas and express them,
I have written countless poems
and published many of them,
I have married a wonderful woman
and spent many good years with her,
and I have seen my son find a cool lady
and raise a delightful daughter.
That I pause to think of more
indicates the place
into which the rest falls.
The meaning,

according to friends,
floats between Jesus saving me
and a kind twist-of-fate;
I am content with science explaining
the electricity of the mind
tracking eye movement,
streaming content in,
and instructing muscles to respond;
the velocity of mass
powered by fossil fuels
on a set trajectory
and changing that path
based on differing impediments;
and the body quickly rerouting nourishment,
like oxygen and nutrients,
as well as reallocating cells
for repair and rebuilding.
Really.
No joke.

# # #

THE LOCKSMITH

Peggy Insula

The locksmith drove around the town;
He opened cars up to a score.
On any given April day,
He might have opened more.

His wife took calls from people stressed,
Bewailing keys they'd locked inside
Or lost upon the beckoning beach
With rising of hypnotic tide.

And so, the locksmith was not surprised
When his wife handed him a note.
"Please come right now to open my house,"
Was the message that Mr. Bear wrote.

The address sent the locksmith far
From his usual rounds 'round town.
When he arrived at the address named,
He bowed his head in a frown.

"This can't be right," the locksmith said.
"This is no residential place,
But to be sure, I'll go inside."
But he ran back out red-faced.

"Brevard County Zoo," the business sign read.
An animal keeper laughed at the note.

Part VII: Fooled Again

"Mr. Bear indeed does live right here,
But we can't let him out, whatever he wrote."

# # #

FOOLED AGAIN

Betty Whitaker Jackson

I thought she was my friend
Until she betrayed my trust.

I thought his love was true
'Til another's he confessed.

I thought my grade was "A"
But the computer recorded "C."

I thought the shrimp was fresh
Until it sickened me.

I thought our land was free
'Til WOKE and CRT

I thought summer break was sacred
'Til yearlong school emerged.

I thought the game was won
But the three-pointer pulled them ahead,

I thought I was done with examples
But April Fool nonsense caught me again.

# # #

APRIL FOOL'S DAY

Nick Kaplan

April Fool's Day is almost here
A time of foolery, friendship, and fear.
The stories a fable
We seek to convince,
The mark, the person, with words to assist
All for a laugh, a smile coerced,
On Aprils Fool's Day,
We're all at our worst.

#

APRIL 1ST

Richard Marshall

'Tis April my love,
and along with the flowers,
'tis the passage of time,
the foibles, the hours!

The hours we've spent,
in the meadows and fields,
in the shallows, and streams,
delighting in nature's, bounteous yields.

Tis' a warm day!
It's sunny! Gosh! I can almost see!
The bluebird is lovely. Spring has arrived!
Misty Monarch hastens. Bonnie Bee makes her honey.

'Tis the first day of April my darlin',
April Fools, the pundits decry.
What's there forever?
What could possibly, go awry!

This durn' visor -
keeps gettin' in my way.
My passenger tells me, to grin, and to bear – after all,
it's all that keeps me, from going astray!

The Java it's perkin',
the hay's golden yellow,

Part VII: Fooled Again

not a bur in my saddle -
could you scoot over, Othello?

# # #

NOT GETTING FOOLED AGAIN

Ashley McGrath

On April Fools' Day,
Folks have tricks they play.
It would be great to photograph
All the stunts that make you laugh.

This day makes some people annoyed.
Funny pranks are hard to avoid.
They always happen on April first.
Don't hold back the laughter, or you'll burst!

# # #

THE BIRTHDAY PRESENT

Noel Sinchak

On the day of my birth, a gift from my mate,
Encased in paper, oh I couldn't wait.
Inside was a tool, not a treasure, to my frown,
A screwdriver, not a jewel or a crown.

Distaste etched my face, hard to hide,
Her joyous chuckle, my disappointment, she spied.
She clarified, with a gleam in her side,
To retrieve my true gift, this tool I'd abide.

I unscrewed an unused cabinet, with the tool in hand,
And inside, a surprise that was grand.
A wooden chess table on a pedestal so fine,
My heart leapt with joy, "This gift is divine!"

Satisfied, she gave me my next task,
To sculpt the chess pieces, a creative mask.
Design them, carve them, make them shine,
In my own time, the chess set was mine.

Though the initial gift had caused dismay,
Her cleverness had brightened my day.
Creating the pieces was worth the while,
Every move on the board made me smile.

# # #

THE SWITCH

Noel Sinchak

During my military tenure, a tale of jest,
A friend of mine made a humorous request.
Bet me twenty-five, with a gleam in his chest,
Said he'd crack my locker open, like a conquest.

Curiosity piqued, I took the bet,
He fiddled with my lock, like a seasoned vet.
Suddenly, it sprung open, as if the code he'd met,
In disbelief, I looked, my face wet with sweat.

Astounded, I asked, how he'd unveiled the code,
He confessed his mischief, in a playful mode.
Swapped his lock for mine, the toad,
Oh, what a prank! His cleverness showed.

In the locker tale, I was the jest,
But in his humor, friendship was expressed.
A reminder of times, in military vest,
Of friendships formed, and memories impressed.

#

TRIANGLE OF HOPE

Noel Sinchak

In my life's journey, I once had a bitter phase,
Battling a divorce, lost in its grim maze.
A faulty Dodge Omni, a shoddy machine,
And a legal dispute with the education scene.

A survival course in far Washington State,
An Air Force training that was my fate.
Yet near it resided, my family kin,
Relatives to see, where do I begin?

Arrived at Fairchild base, days before the start,
Caught up with my kin, a warmth in my heart.
The city boy in me, in awe of the mountains,
A serenity flows, like peaceful fountains.

The sunny day turned to a storm's dark reign,
Inside the car, I sat with my camera in vain.
Beside a water body, a sight caught my eye,
In the pitch-dark sky, a triangle pried.

Opened it did, to reveal clouds so white,
Specks of blue, in a beautiful light.
Sunlight kissed the mountain's edge,
Illuminating the water with a silvery pledge.

In despair's throes, such a vision was rare,
A beacon of hope, light in despair.

Part VII: Fooled Again

Yet, as quickly as it came, it receded,
Back into darkness, where hope was needed.

Such a day, I believe, changed my life's song,
A tiny glimpse of hope made me strong.
Up the path of despair, I began to tread,
Towards light from darkness, I was led.

Nature's tricks, so profound and wise,
Taught me to seek, the beautiful in disguise.
This was the start of my resilient spree,
The birth of courage, in the heart of me.

This tale I share, with you in stride,
May your journeys be filled with pride.
Seek nature's beauty, let hope unfurl,
As you traverse through your world.

# # #

Precious Publishing Academy – May 6, 2023

12:30pm - 2:00pm at the West Melbourne Public Library

Technology, the Art of Writing, and the Business of Publishing

Precious Publishing
www.PreciousPublishing.biz

Academy

Anthology Alliance

CTS Press

• Courses   • Webinars   • Workshops

Poetry – Showers & Flowers

Showers fall from the sky
Dancing drops of liquid grace from high

Flowers raise their grateful heads
Petals funnel water's welcome call to beds

Showers bring life to the earth
Flowers give life its color and worth

Les averses et les fleurs
Gervais Trottier (2023)

The saying "April showers bring May flowers" is a common proverb that suggests that the rain showers in April lead to the growth and blooming of flowers in May. For those living in northern climates, it implies that even though April might be a wet and dreary month, it's necessary for the beauty and growth that follows in May. The saying is a reminder that the natural world operates on a cycle and that the difficult times are an essential part of the process of growth and renewal.

***

Scott Tilley is president of Precious Publishing, an emeritus professor at the Florida Institute of Technology, president and founder of the Center for Technology & Society, president and co-founder of Big Data Florida, a member of the Florida Writers Association Board of Directors, and a Space Coast Writers' Guild Fellow. His recent books include *AFTERMATH* (2022), *PETS* (2021), *Systems Analysis & Design* (2020), and *Technical Justice* (2019). He holds a Ph.D. in computer science from the University of Victoria.

www.PreciousPublishing.biz/join

FLOWERS AND SHOWERS

Christopher Robin Adams

Some blooms arrived,
then shriveled and died;
the dry ground
forced
the county to issue a "no burn" directive;
somewhere in here,
as spring sat with a flat tire elsewhere,
a cold snap zapped the first young green.
Then rain stepped in, fell in,
and poured like it was raining,
and flooded and flooded
and washed and cleansed all
but our hearts,
that were still asleep
        after another night of frogs:
the poor and homeless and hungry
still cannot find an apartment,
the black and brown
continue to venture out at risk,
and wealthy haves
continue to pull gates closed and lock them.

When the world
backwards itself,
do we turn to growing wisdom
and ask "why?"
or do we reach for a god

and cry "why me?"

Then the rain arrived.
Lightly.
Water levels are far below normal.
We wait for more rain;
since it is typically accompanied by hurricane winds,
we are stuck with a cliché:
"Be careful what you wish for."

We know why the world
somersaults,
we understand why it weathers events
differently
now than in centuries before,
     but we have chosen an easier route:
     eat an éclair.

We may have flowers
for a bit,
We may have a bit
of showers,
but Cassandra tells us
with data and photographs and suffering
what will come;
we prefer the éclair.

#

BEWARE OF FLOWERS

Peggy Insula

A glorious, cream-colored magnolia bloom
Was calling to me to have a peek.
I drew so close that its delicate petals
Tickled me teasingly on the cheek.
Enraptured and drunk with its sweet, Southern scent,
I just didn't see the bumblebee
That sharpstung me on my inquisitive nose
And angrily buzzed away from me.
My eyes fast swelled shut; my nose grew a large lump;
My luck had run out—no help was nigh.
I coughed and wheezed and with no EpiPen near,
I knew for sure I was going to—
PLOP!

# # #

FLORIDA SNOWFLOWERS

Peggy Insula

O Lord, how I love the Florida snow!
Six-petaled stars no bigger than a dime
with centers of gold,
They grow in clusters and expand to blankets
that cover the lawn.
They need no bitter cold or chilling wind—
Only the bright winter Florida sun
Produces this breathtaking bounty of tiny lush blooms.
Welcome! I love you!

# # #

SHOWERS AND FLOWERS

Betty Whitaker Jackson

When I'm depressed
I plant marigolds to brighten my spirits
And chase the blues away.

When I celebrate
I plant orchids
And rejoice in their beauty.

When I mourn
I plant roses
For everlasting fragrance.

When it rains
I plant resurrection lilies
Pink beauty only after showers.

When I honor veterans
I plant red carnations
Remembering shed blood.

When I see desolation
I plant grasses
To cover loss.
When I worship
I choose lilies
The resurrection symbol.

Part VIII: Showers & Flowers

When I think romance
I choose daisies'
Happy and free.

When it's spring
I plant pansies
Sweet faces of joy.

When winter's too old
I want crocus, and tulips and daffodils
To break through frozen sod.

When I think aromas
Lilacs and jasmine
Come to mind.

And when my walls are bare
I hang flowers paintings
Of every possible hue
In thanksgiving for God's
Generosity and love of created beauty.

# # #

SPRINGTIME

Nick Kaplan

Ah springtime, when the color's the thing.
The blooms burst forth and the tiny birds sing.
With a spade and shovel, we dare to create,
The magistery of nature and then we await,

The rain and the sunlight, so precious and new,
For the bees and the pollen and the flowers too.
The butterflies flutter, and the seedlings do grow,
The snow starts to melt, and the streams now flow.

The trees all show their green color and yet,
The sneezing, the coughing, the eyes getting wet,
The mending, the dusting, the cleanings a chore,
The painting, the shopping, the garden, and more.

The dander, the hornets, and the bugs populate,
With the mission of finding a suitable mate.
The Ivy, the lotion and the snakes explore,
The rabbits, the squirrels, and the flies galore,

The hope for renewal and life to beget,
Ah! The splendor of springtime, boy, it's hard to forget.

#

TESTIMONY OF SPRING

Richard Marschall

Clouds of confusion test man's faculties.
and he is held captive, to his delusions!
He sits high, on his pedestal of academia –
time hovers, on our brother's, grim reality!
Like the harsh wind that roils the bubbling sea,
like the lioness protecting her cubs,
mortals lash out, at that which they do not know,
coveting perfection, as the vine, to the tree.
Mind you, the darkness pre-shadows the dawn,
and the arctic winter, the antecedent of Spring!
Everything cometh, if we only, hold on!
The testimony of Spring, its quintessence of life,
the blessed awakening of the unblemished fawn,
the certainty, the miracle, of rebirth and life!

# # #

TRELLISED TOWERS

Richard Marschall

Trellised towers of primrose and delicate lily,
arousing our senses, like the arabicas of Spring,
false pretenses and guises, in maiden's attire,
strung carelessly on their wooden frames, willy nilly.
Life's little bumps fain to wanton preclusion,
mortal recitations, dressing the staid halls, of
academia's finest hours, and learned thoughts -
the magician's illusions, and man's allusions.
Man can only strive for the perfection that is his.
No amount of deceit, can ever mask this goal, and
there is no shelter in the heavens, for that which is!
Like the colorful lily that has no regret,
like the fast-moving rivulet that creates all the fizz,
our mettle will be tested, time and again!

# # #

SHOWERS LEAD TO FLOWERS

Ashley McGrath

Winter finally comes to an end
When temperatures upward trend.
Spring is the season when showers
Bring up many plants and flowers.

Several days of rain and sunshine
Lead to a colorful ground design.
Flora of various hues
Are seen in beautiful views.

# # #

FLORIDA SPRINGSHINE

Linda Paul

Spring is here in my Florida yard
But this year, unlike the last
I have killed the chiggers off with poison
My itching ankle days are past.

Joyfully, I go outdoors
Into my yard, bite-free
Hoping to have a garden
After I kill that pepper tree.

After I pull all the stickers
After the vine with thorns is dead
After I hack off the lower fronds
Of Sabal palm that hit my head.

The weeds grow high
But my lawn guy can't mow
The afternoon rains keep him away
But the monthly bill is still a go.

Spring is here in my Florida yard
Summer sometimes starts in Spring
If I don't plant my garden at Christmas
I will not harvest one damn thing.

# # #

INTELLIGENT GARDENING

Linda Paul

I contemplate my black thumb
And my Florida garden so brown and dry
If only, as in poetry
My yard could be tended by AI.

#

LIFE'S PASSION SPRINGING

Carol Schweitzer

In all living things, passion's hum does weave,
From a singular source, its essence conceived.
With love's mighty force, on comet tails it rides,
DNA's joyous song, where molecular delight abides.

In waves of bliss, seeds surge in flight,
To earth or womb, in darkness or light.

A new green stalk, a leaf's design unfurls,
Upwards it strains, 'til concrete's grip it hurls.
With passion's drive, survival it embraces,
Seed's sacrifice, new growth it chases.

# # #

SHOWERS AND FLOWERS

Carol Schweitzer

Droplets fall softly
Raining God's luscious food
Thirsty leaves, gratitude

Petals gulp liquid
Rich soil feeding roots
Of green shoots.

Divine provision, magic nutrients
Morphs into flower-popping hues
Scrumptious rainbows - yellow, orange, pink, and blue.

Petals' perfumes sent to be breathed
Take wafting air-rides
To spread gratefulness to noses and eyes.

Flowers are grateful
To end their deep craving
We, too, seek showers for saving.

# # #

FLOWERS

Noel Sinchak

From a six-hour journey, through the sky's might,
Tired and weary, in the softening night,
But a new place calls, before sleep's gentle bite,
An explorer at heart, in the pale moonlight.

A meal consumed, attire changed with speed,
A stroll I ventured, curiosity's feed.
In time, a spectacle, too strange to believe,
A sight so alien, one could scarcely conceive.

A cactus stood, alone in the Arctic's fold,
In Thule, Greenland, a tale to be told.
Seven fifty miles from the Arctic's cold hold,
Nine hundred more, to the North pole, bold.

A photo snapped, at the midnight hour,
In stark silence, under a sky's cold bower.
Ordinary, yet in this place, it had power,
A testament to life, a desert flower.

No other green did my eyes trace,
On my path back, to my resting space.
Mother Nature's jest, a curious embrace,
Surprises sprung, in the strangest place.

# # #

SHOWERS

Noel Sinchak

Fresh from basic, as a loadmaster deemed,
A flight I sought, my heart in mission teemed,
My superior nodded, his answer was keen,
To the sky above, in a craft of machine.

"Showers and flowers," a phrase of delight,
Rain then sun, then blooms bright in the light.
Yet winds can howl, and lightning ignite,
In the tempest's power, I found a new sight.

From McGuire AFB, our flight would begin,
To Torrejon AB, amidst the sky's din.
A hiccup occurred, radar fell to whim,
We returned to McGuire, safety through hymn.

In memory echoed a tale of dire cost,
A radar-less flight, in the UK storm tossed.
Disintegrated in air, eighteen souls lost,
A poignant reminder, in our minds embossed.

Fixed and ready, we soared to the air,
To Lajes Field, crew's rest awaited there.
Thunderstorms en route, a spectacle rare,
In the storm's dance of lightning, I could only stare.

Vertically, horizontally, diagonally it raced,
A celestial marvel, in the sky it traced,

Part VIII: Showers & Flowers

Never into a thunderstorm, such peril faced,
Respect and caution, firmly embraced.

Landed at Lajes, the night to regain,
Next day to Spain, then back again.
First mission complete, experience gained,
Respect for storms, in my heart ingrained.

Yet nature's wrath, has a gentle side,
After the storm, a rainbow does reside.
Beauty transcends, destruction's tide,
A balance of contrasts, in the skies wide.

# # #

FLORIDA GARDENING, MAY FLOWERS

Darci Wolcott

As I entered yoga class this morning
a conversation was in process
Was I the woman with
Compromised knees?
Yes, that would be me

Whereupon a kind stranger
Handed me a knee pad for class
It had lettering: "Gardening:
Bloom where you're planted"
As it happened, we had

A magnificent crop
Of dandelions this winter
Our yard was filled with wishes
Ready to be blown about
By the first good wind — or
Perhaps a passing toddler
Whose mother encouraged
His curiosity while

Nearby — probably — a ridiculous
Ibis was dirtying his pink/orange
Beak probing for bugs
In our so-called lawn

Part VIII: Showers & Flowers

A determined firebush is enveloping
Our yellow and green tri-tip hedge
Seeding as it grows, its red flowers
Competing with wind-borne
Hot-pink periwinkles which
Had a head start with the

Extra rain we had last month
Our sandspurs are flourishing
It's all a ravishing green to me —
Just don't go barefoot

Perhaps you think me lazy
(Not far from the truth I guess)
But how prescient my generous yoga
Classmate was! The perfect present
For my body, mind and spirit
(Not to mention knees)

"Bloom Where You're Planted"
Why not? You can't blow a wish
From a pampered peony.

# # #

ABOUT THE POETS

Christopher Robin ("Kit") Adams, a prolific writer since 1958, has seen his stories, essays, and poems published internationally. His poetry, celebrated in readings across Missouri and Florida, complements his distinguished career in English education, including National Board Certification and a role with the National Writing Project. Retired from teaching, Kit remains active as a Lifetime Member of the Space Coast Writers' Guild and President of Brevard Scribblers. His debut poetry collection, *Spanish Cedar: Preserving the ART of the Cigar Experience*, was published in 2014. He continues to mentor through the UCF Florida Writing Project.

Peggy Ball, hailing from New York and Connecticut, published her first poem in fourth grade. Her poetry, essays, and stories have been featured in various publications and earned accolades from notable organizations, including the Space Coast Poetry Club, National League of Pen Women, Strawbridge Art League, and Brevard Scribblers. Peggy has authored five books: *Tickle Toe Hill; The Many Moods of Love; 50-50, The Mini Saga Book; Florida Souvenir;* and *What Do You Wish For?* Residing in Merritt Island, Florida, she draws inspiration from the local wildlife, including dolphins and manatees.

Helen Bennett, from Brooklyn, New York, has authored eight books spanning poetry, humanism, and a memoir. A retired librarian, editor, and English teacher at both high school and college levels, she has spent the last nineteen years teaching at Senior Adventures in Learning (SAIL) in Brevard County, Florida. A Unitarian Universalist and Humanist since 1995, Helen holds degrees from Brooklyn College (Phi Beta Kappa), the University of Wisconsin, the University of California at Berkeley, and Florida Atlantic University.

Peggy Insula has published the novels *Letters to Uncle Jeb*, *Murder Runs in my Family*, *Choices*, and the novellas *Just Murder, Sudsy*, *How Not to Steal a Car*, and *You're Nobody Till Somebody Kills You*. *Waiting Rooms* recounts her husband's cancer diagnosis and treatment. Fictional characters and events add humor to this otherwise daunting journey. *Chamomile Poems, Travels with Ninny and Zander, All the Dogs I've Loved Before*, and three anthologies complete her works.

Betty Whitaker Jackson, a retired language arts teacher, has written numerous books in several genres: devotional guides, memoirs, fiction, poetry, and children's books, and has written hundreds of "My Psalms," honoring the format of Biblical Psalms. She has been published in twelve anthologies and won first prize in the Reader's Digest Life-Rich Memoir contest for her book *Rocking Chair Porch: Summers with Grandma*. She volunteers with the Space Coast Symphony Orchestra and the Covenant Church in Palm Bay, FL. Her website is www.bettyjackson.net

Tim Janecke, originally from Minnesota, where he grew up playing hockey, transitioned into a fulfilling career as an elementary school teacher in Florida. Married with no children, Tim has recently cultivated a new interest in poetry, initially sparked by his attempts at writing song lyrics. This newfound passion has led him to explore other artistic avenues, including a budding interest in acting, enriching his creative endeavors. Engaging with other writers and absorbing their work as part of this project has been an exhilarating experience, opening new worlds of expression and connection for him.

Nick Kaplan has short stories published in *PANDEMIC, PETS,* and *AFTERMATH.* He has written essays for the Brevard Scribblers anthologies *Driftwood, Written in the Sun,* and *Christmas.* He is a Space Coast Writers Guild member and contributed to their poetry anthology *Horizons.* His novel *The Long Game* (under the pen name Nicholas Taylor) is a 21st-century story of espionage and government corruption. He is retired and lives in Florida.

Richard Marschall received his B.S. degree from Townson University and performed postgraduate work at Western Illinois University. His short stories have been published in anthologies from the Space Coast Writers' Guild and the Brevard Scribblers. His poems have appeared in publications by Poetry Soup and Eber & Wein. He served as Literary Editor of the Brevard Scribblers for 2018-2019.

Ashley McGrath is a quality analyst for J. Lodge, a Cognosante company. Ashley, a University of Central Florida alumna, published her autobiography *UnabASHed by Disability* in 2014. Her writing has appeared in online columns, a disability blog, local publications, and several anthologies. She is a Lifetime Member of the Space Coast Writers' Guild, a Director-at-Large, and the Don Argo Award coordinator. She is active at her church in Palm Bay, Florida.

Linda Paul is a writer and musician based in Melbourne, Florida. Her monologue *Semper Fi* was performed on stage and TV in Portland, Oregon. Her play *Halloween in the ICU* was a finalist in the Midwest Dramatists Center Conference 2018. She has published poems, essays, and a memoir in *The Oregonian* newspaper and the Brevard Scribblers anthologies *Driftwood* and *Written in the Sun*. Her article *Finding Henry* was published in the Alabama Genealogical Society magazine (AGS), and her short story *Seventh Sister* was published on Amazon. She teaches ukulele at the Eau Gallie Public Library.

Carol Schweitzer, transitioning from a successful career in business development and community leadership, is embarking on a creative journey as an aspiring writer and poet. Her rich professional experience, characterized by strategic thinking and adept relationship-building, lays a solid foundation for her literary pursuits. Carol's venture into the arts reflects her commitment to personal growth and her passion for exploring new modes of expression. This blend of business acumen with newfound artistic ambition underscores her desire to inspire and connect with others.

Noel Sinchak served in the US Air Force and was stationed in Florida and Germany. After completing military service, he worked as a substitute teacher for seventh-grade social studies while attending Rutgers University night school. He then joined the US Air Force Reserve as a qualified loadmaster, leading to a federal civil service career. He served in various positions and was stationed in numerous locations in the United States and the United Kingdom. He lives in Florida.

Darci Wolcott, a retired teacher and mental health counselor, has recently embraced the world of poetry, joining the vast community of amateur poets and enriching her lifelong passions for reading, travel, and playing chamber music. She and her husband have made Indialantic, Florida, their home for over sixty years, where they enjoy the vibrant local culture and the natural beauty of their surroundings.

Poems of the Moment

ABOUT THE EDITOR

Scott Tilley is president and founder of Precious Publishing, an emeritus professor at the Florida Institute of Technology, president of the Center for Technology & Society, president of Big Data Florida, a member of the Board of Directors of the Florida Authors and Publishers Association, and a Space Coast Writers' Guild Fellow. His recent books include *AFTERMATH* (2022), *PETS* (2021), *Systems Analysis & Design* (2020), and *Technical Justice* (2019). He holds a Ph.D. in computer science from the University of Victoria.

Poems of the Moment

PRECIOUS POETRY

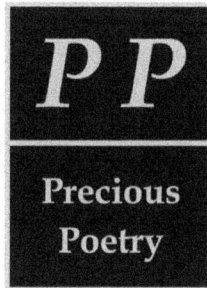

Words are important. Poems are the ultimate reflection of the art and craft of writing in a unique style designed by the poet and pleasing to the reader. Precious Poetry publishes books of poems that delight and refresh. If you want to assemble and publish a poetry collection, contact us!

Precious Poetry is an imprint of Precious Publishing, LLC. Precious Publishing specializes in taking your writing ideas from conception to fruition. We know that your stories are precious to you, and we'll do everything we can to help you see your work published.

All our books are available online from Amazon.com, usually in print and Kindle formats. You are the author, we are the editor and publisher, and the world's biggest bookstore is the global distributor.

http://www.PreciousPublishing.biz/PreciousPoetry

Poems of the Moment

WRITTEN IN TIME

Scott Tilley

In fleeting moments, verbs take flight,
A dance of ink in the soft moonlight,
Each verse a pulse, a heartbeat's sound,
In life's vast tapestry, stories are found.

These poems capture time's swift flow,
In whispered hues of joy and woe,
Moments treasured, lost, then found,
In woven words, our thoughts are bound.

FIN